Slaves to Do These Things

Amy King

Slaves to Do These Things

Amy King

BlazeVOX [books]

Buffalo, New York

Slaves to Do These Things by Amy King
Copyright © 2009

Published by BlazeVOX [books]

Printed in the United States of America

Book design by Geoffrey Gatza
Cover art by Orna Ben-Shoshan

First Edition
ISBN 10 : 9781935402312
Library of Congress Control Number: 2009925613

BlazeVOX [books]
303 Bedford Ave
Buffalo, NY 14216

Editor@blazevox.org

publisher of weird little books

BlazeVOX [books]

blazevox.org

2   4   6   8   0   9   7   5   3   1

B   X

Acknowledgements

Many thanks to the editors of the following publications, in which these poems, or versions of them, originally appeared: *Aufgabe, Del Sol Review, Denver Syntax, Diode, Dusie, Fogged Clarity, Fiera Lingue, Marsh Hawk Review, Moria Poetry, Pirene's Fountain, Siren: A Literary and Art Journal, Unlikely Stories, Welter, Wheelhouse Magazine, Web Del Sol,* and *With + Stand.*

My gratitude also to Ana Bozicevic, Michael Steinman, Carolyn and Don Benfer, and Geoffrey Gatza for their encouragement and steady support.

Contents

Act IV

Act V

Conceive me as a dream of stone:
my breast, where mortals come to grief,
is made to prompt all poets' love,
mute and noble as matter itself.

—Charles Baudelaire, "Beauty"

Slaves to Do These Things

Act I

The soul that suffered from being its body...

THE PSALMS CALLED "BREATH"

I came out twice
sobered and married,
then aimless and pregnant.
My shin splints against
the head of my bed
while the room spins
the arms of sensation
around my waist, my torso,
my bosom now suckling
the world's new adults, mostly male
and lost, back to what
it must be like to nurture
the neglect of a virginal
mother the church would have us
buy out. Mother Mary, O contrary,
why do you never exist? Why
the business of insisting
a fear of eternal flames
from hollow fangs that
would render the spirit deaf?
Our love flowers the cockroach
of death into augured cues
of eggplant eyes,
strangled to be alive. We play life
until delivered, and then
turn swirling puddles
of earthworm guts
into every cell the boots collect
by the steps
of soldiers, teachers
and journalists. We are everywhere
terrorists, suicide failures, half-

rolled against the fence of a homeless
drifter, beaten dirt knapsacks
to carry our buttons and heat.
We warm up north and cool by
the Midwestern moon.
We peyote for fullness and eat
cameras to claim the mercy
of a bacterial armpit safari.
We stretch against the office boxes
that cloister us apart,
buying puppy mill dogs
to escape the screens of the daily
randomness of order.
A tongue at the foot cleanses
the sole to prepare
for desert-like journey.
Let us prepare then, for
I believe in your winter
and the summer it stirs,
I believe in the lamb that lies
by the fold of your elbow,
I hold to confusion
that this space is blank, though
not intentionally so. It is so
because you are not yet in it,
though you are here with
your eyes, which exist,
taking all grammars in, as I omit.

FAILED TO INCLUDE

Not quite as chilly today
as it is tomorrow
upon your return
to the city where
you slay me, you slave me—
& I begin to wait. I wait on you,
your every necessity
and dream-blown romance.

Ed Berrigan walks jobless
to eggs at Blue Bella diner,
Ana visits her last grandfather
Croatia-bound, they eat annual
lamb on a spit
while I lather here, up and down
stairs, serving you
crunchy treats and cleaning
your limbs from their sap.

Ben Evans makes New York
plays from his lake-side hotel
in Muskegon, Frightened Rabbit sings
for the kindergarten class,
who dances a religion
only kids still grasp, and I wait
for the mail that never
comes to pass. You stay,
ghost pagan present.

Next day, Tracy and Julian
supply us all night
with an endless horn of salad

and banter, plenty of wines
and vibes to ferment
perishable grey matter.
We speak in dog voices.
We leave, home-full & spent.

Now, a year before
the end of the war, Claude
Cahun began
her literary studies. She
wrote the very first
lecture she heard, Lucy Renee's
"Essence of the Tragic"
attended in the company
of fellow students,
all of them persons
with war injuries.
She culled her amputee notes.

The suicides stood
experiments; we became a part
of the kitten
background, wallpaper mists
of who held what
body cut with what flesh
desired and parched in the name
of what fascist cause in this day
and country would allow that brand
of you must be the better
me fundamental song.

She found in her studies
wanderlust and through the lens
of never betrothed,
"I belong: suffer double,

molding my other one."
Kerry and Miller stand with wings
for the gusts of slaves
discovered to descend
that we had intermingled two
other settings: mask & friend.

Cindy, Nan, and Diane brought
the humming photographs
to beds, window closets,
that the seeds of the kingdom
come from the pupil. Prison dilated
CC's alter she, ushered
chameleon people of the female
to cradles, through kitchens
and the iris, backwashing the tomb.

Frida saw they wanted
the sun by the angle of our table,
our desire to be parents
—of any living thing— slipping
through bamboo backs
into soup puddles: we ladled.
Do you have an ending
called, "Why the wetness of a cup?"
Gazpacho warms,
sangria slurs, and we stand
to leave by the town's outskirts:
Malaga, New York, Tehran, Budapest.

Longer by land, we follow the counsel
of a sundial's advantage:
through the backlit terrain of ear canals.
We make melodies that ring
the scalp of dirt lots and sand

shells fixed on translation to what
is palpable: sirens who hold
a kind of sight with strong tones,
audible diamonds that cut.

Until we walk with the spine
of poster-child lips, we suck dew-
drops off pewter, sour the wine,
shake the harbor's sinew,
kick crumbs from pale shoulders,
and shoot bottle rockets of faltering
love. We swell and precede,
lit to age the coming America.

THE MEMORY SKIN

I am opposite marriage.
My dinner cake is made
guerrilla style. Getting in
their faces sly,
shotgun raw, we spoke.
You held me well until
you closed with
the intellectual integrity
of a fucked-up life. To give
in to the grace
of a sudden condition,
that is the primacy of thought.

My first false encounter came
with the blue eye of a mother,
forward swimming
the foreign gravity of a father,
deadpan cigar smoke,
rehashed cement sounds,
turning water.
Take up my flour,
soak my skin
with the limbs of vermouth:
the ear wouldn't
hear any louder
the cries of Platonic plans
cave-bound. I too am cavernous,
ready to swallow the first
sign of finger to point
or hubris as needle.

Stitch me clean, remove
the fist from your saddle

and steer me
with the sweet sweat
of birth. That is,
in the scent that
there is no light, I
can see every
artificial flame:
people in Paris
and Zanzibar cutting
garlic in half
for rainbow
trout caught by the poles
of their own hands,
arms
that stretch through static
memories not yet their own,
but that of the imperialist
retching
to make what last
was never theirs
to behold.
Now scoop her here,
listen to the sea's shell
repeat a fish-like
backbone
breaking, your teeth
at the innards of life.

SURVIVAL OF THE FITTEST

The philosopher, a pompadour,
speaks without moving his lips.
He throws
a cannonball, like caution,
about like a voluptuary,
which means there is an object
seen at great distance
wearing its garments
for slip-to-lace to shrug-it-off,
much like the love we offer
departed cast members
who always showered
a licking smile
your way as you passed
out. Forgive me, I am the final
seminary soul to
check your shape
in the dress of that embalming line—
The fundamental issue here
doesn't seem to be about speed
but about whose process
I repeat
well enough to say average
grim reapers would sleep
and very few good ones go eager
to eat the lice from your hands,
pass the soup of stupidity
off as love's
castigations, which goes without
saying are just the feathers
in childhood's cap that float
behind his every footstep
slapping him back
through bathroom lines
until the ship sets sail,

never to be heard
from beyond the equator's
jungle-rife scenes and slaves
we earlier made but no
longer cohabit with,
or mark the imprint
of our footprints against.
It's not a complicated math.
Add the pressure of expectation
to the height of expectation.
Weigh cooperation
against the fear of an adult persuasion.
Where does it look like
everything comes from?
I want to meet the woman who
pulled that clock
by its gnarly roots and offered
throttled seconds
sideways through the mouth
of a vagina, through the lips
of her species
that refuses the periphery
until every body asks why
not. I am those numbers,
that bidding, those
sevens in the armpits
and zeros dancing snake eyes.
My ones are tied on
to the brick of my revolving
heart's axis, presumed
whole numbers gone missing.
Shadowed by the nagging
hope is that we women
will prepare the canal
for you to slip back through & into.
Such is the plight of the dodo,
staring down the barrel,
demanding life to speak.

THIS COFFIN'S BUCKET OF SOIL

All around your face, eggs
buffed glass eyes
to the point of shine.

Suspended with such
wide gulf,
timed marrow,
we swim toward sharks together.

We climb the organ's insides
like helmsmen dancing thunder,
a tooth biting down
the street that pierces
the row-boated brain.

The organ shudders her great lung
nestled in sotto voce,
digesting grief through the bodies'
voids, trimmed with wind.

They tell me nothing's gone.

That I can see the air
that isn't skinning me.
That I can dive further without
this coffin's bucket of soil &
hold to the leg's quick dead dust,
each scripture,
wherever the foot goes ghost.

MIRACLE ON THE HUDSON

Buried by midnight
I am a warm
fly in amber.

A reflection buzzes
against my wings'
vision quest:
this window square
above the Atlantic,
leading me down the lane
by moonlight's hand
beneath the shadow's sun
in oil-blue water,
a darker planetary hug
of crooked limb
with etched-on hand.

You have not listened
to the tones of trees,
our branches, our trunks,
calm as axes,
gathered roots beneath
a sheer drop of future stars,
at least.

We flicker too,
stone-white skeletons
modeled on the earth's
black-bloated heart,
her skinny boots
that march circles
on the universe.

We go around in them,
meeting ourselves
behind our backs,
knocking the boney
knockers of spines
with parading breath.

One side strikes
the other: language cheapens?

We speak where all symbols
want power
such as a door which opens,
takes persimmons to its lover,
the other side, to no knock.
We can't remind the lover
to love any more
than we can love ourselves
without the lover,
borne by the landing of light.

Act II

Growing up spoiled a lot of things.

THE ALWAYS SONG

The month is April.
Writing from an old house
in front of a prairie and
a forest whose name
walks through tall brown grass,
I could say
much about the part of not knowing,
its aisles
of tracks and traps, temptations
that charm with wooden waves
of ceilinged sight.
But I am savage, outside.
Never once did pools of light
sway this way.
In aubergine moons, I lift
the width of my wrists, I hallelujah
a terrible god, raining
bits of paper
turned to lost voodoo and orchestras
until I come of age,
smothered by years of breaking loose
clouds of longing against
every loyal thing,
measuring wildness by the muddy sky
I stood beside, to this night.

COWS

Her moon was a heavy
teacup,
lifted light at the rim
by fainting stars &
milkweed impulse
to smell her hair within.

The cows shock
those of us closest
in clover.

I take my flashlight,
approach the pasture
and lay
your beautiful face
in darkness.

Turning to me,
turning to girls
we were sudden, innocent,
and
ready-made
for how, because
they were not,
we switched
the thrills of water
to powdered wine,
put on my best-dressed
mandible and bit
into the sink
of her left cheek.

Quiet with eyes,
could I explain
anything at all—
by the night
of the rain
I sparrow, then fall.

STIMULUS PACKAGE

I come for you on the people's chariot
interpreted in nightgown,
sidelined and smoking,
breakfast huevos in hand,
for we are poorer figures with lust,
and poorer still, talking this city
from block into block into
that which sells
a plastic surprise
in the snake oil's morning,
a unisex of truth bearing.
She rears her head into mine
for the waking bile
onto newsprint hands
that speak into being
god's pretty linemen.   They
are petty, those granite masters
of needlepoint. They serve
to handle the butterflies' scratch
on dawn's aching shores,
another sexual intercourse. We lean
and lap the streams of coffees
and cream, milky caramels
that blow the kiss of hellos
into bombs overflowing
fast, jasmine
blossom masks that make
the toxins' provinces
burn our angular bodies.
We stand for bleached blonde
smiles of names
on next summer's shores.
We play bikini faces, and
though the walls remain intact,
we ignore the dress of death
when they mirage America back.

BE GOOD AND BE COUNTRY

When the grapes are in their wrath, I lie
low in my headless socket to see your faces
through age's predictable reading glass.
The same electron can be in two places at once.
From that death, I open the cask that restrains
your paralysis breath.
I want to rescue you from this toy chest,
but I won't use my only gusto, so
here I reside, cocker spaniel vacuum packed,
crooked brain, crustacean waves of danger.
Look backwards. You've got your circular jaw,
you've got a circular youth with suicide glimmer,
even the age of honeycomb corpses;
people love to bet your next axe
tells more welts designed to replicate
tattoos of other countries on our backsides.
In fact, you don't hurt grass or beetles
when you stand in vitro; you'd probably
win the hormone race if I pushed you back
in bed, then down the stairs of copulation.
But I'd rather wrestle your entire corpus
than fuck someone for the sake of holes
that empty after me and footnotes
that fuel the rolling whites of your ripe-
eyed torso, applauding its seeded limbo.

BROOKLYN WHITE PARTY

Shame in everything, a dying attention,
to become brave is shame too.
Can they finally engineer birds and bugs
that consume paper and twine
to reduce the size of fake nests
and debris that kills off the lilies?
Your concave thoughts:
you never leave me alone where
I could be utterly alone
within you.
The train flows overhead,
heard between bourbon, elbows,
cheap sidewalk cedar trees,
beneath this overpass with skaters
who bump thuggish flights at mid-night.
We're almost city
except I hallucinate you in the backs of women
carrying a tree home from some holiday
party looking thoroughly leopard
with fish meat in maw and hand-
painted toes, flickers of smoke's butt
off the rim of your life, white wine
in uninsured faces so that
others hope you're vulnerable too—
I know from the taste of memory's slag
just how singular you go,
I parted the seas of geese
and smelled whalebone
for luck, seizing the best organs of myself
each time you came, your orgasms
in the power of this little life's death
and its far-from-bleeding timeframe.

But you don't know how
much you love
the sun until you find
you're dying beneath it, your death
behind the bedpan's fingers
crushing vinegar from blood
into some other lovely thing
within a commandment's voice,
the fall unfolding
turning to lamb, a reindeer's cousin
scared the celebration's over,
the hunters gone home.

Act III

Selling one's soul to God: is to betray the Other.

THE FEAR OF HOPE IS ALSO BEAUTIFUL

On horseback mixing math with philosophy,
her skin is tired,
she is nervous, a never-ending boy,
the kind with soundproof eyes that echo
the faint hymn hers persuades
the hand toward
you with. Prick goes the fingertip,
when she knocks more dents
with a ball-peen hammer
in the sides of your soul.
You know that the punctured
effect is only so that
God can grasp you better
when your feet leave the ground,
you fall in love,
holding hard to the slim slack jaw
of his readymade arms, and brother,
you're all his, dinners out
and hot in the loft,
lots of milked black coffee, croissants,
hair cuttings, cancelled appointments,
and cruising stars
for their place on the ship's bow.
Leaning into backdrafts just to glow,
a silk tongue along the slip
of your underbelly.
You are deadline. You are at most
old fashioned.
You are the tall wheat grass
of commercial voids.
You turn center of the root cellar's
dark damp moist.
And I linger here, like lingering

is everywhere,
taking in the burnt-out air,
sucking spring
from her allergens that would have me
for her very savior, should she feel
the knee of missing a place
in the chorus line lifting
a dress to reveal the shapes
of my opinion exposing her.
The fear of hope is also beautiful
as we tread along
finding several sharks
swimming in place.
To combat the brutality of eyes
that take in these sights,
why don't you tug at the knots
of your wrist with your teeth
and say amen to all of the above,
draw the shades aside and lean
below the waist,
wrapped in cloudless curtains
where we will bathe in the salts
of an iron water, swollen
awake with all that hurts us.

DOCTOR STARCH

He didn't attempt the back door
when I put on my pill box hat,
cautious ingrate.
Sap for what the disease remaindered –
every day left over, I'm gaining
a weight that stands gallows-punched:
& you should, pounds told, eat more,
kill pill, stretch on, walk dogs,
little tongue, stone's throw, vomit up,
grow heart, ask legs, quiver gut,
shake down, no meat, sex less,
prove life, launch death, sell self,
machine me, x ray, honey mound,
pubic eyes, smoke pipe, victim beef,
stare lips, blanket I, apple chunk,
tea bag, growl pouch, pound out,
sea sick, salt off, flesh sag,
liver dip, bile wish, throw soap,
row out, hope vest, that's all
I know, dyed rose, spoon light.

EVERYTHING HAPPENS AT ONCE

The phone sings,
the door knocks,
the government wants their money,
retirement shrinks its future,
I am stuck at the bottom of alert
that is only a test
of what? My wills,
my steel, my permanent enamel?
My memoir remains afloat in a sea of skunk
even as I sink my teeth
into Jennifer Baszile's.
What should I tell you that you don't
already think
you have the right to know?
The tongue's dog is a spongy mop across
my middle toe, which is a lanky thing
meant to prop me up against
gravity's slow-motion heart.
I too have a slower goal;
everyone has already married,
borne babies, executed
their enemies, fixed their failures,
mended frost's fences,
torn the radiators
from their non-working lungs,
replaced the light bulbs
with fireflies and retreated to caves
of this smell onto that hand,
pheromones and glycerin,
shaded beds with grapes to feed you,
the lightning dims,
I'm on your knees, pressing backward,
doing things

I've never watched like
houses in swollen grass, this sloughing off
of perfect muscle
tones so that I immerse in tallness,
flowers and soap
from my fortune's dial tone,
the song of all decay and niceness
to presently tap your shoulder,
take your hand
and rub this lip with the scent
of your rough head,
your heart, your east, but
no such love goes simultaneous,
fleeting forward while God's little mice
gnaw beneath the wooden
four-poster, the fields of water crocus
set adrift with handmade paddles,
human fins, even if this rubble is
drowning buildings
with memories of men
leaping from flames, diving in
the grip of eyeballs,
foods that fill out every pore
still trying to hold to—I mean,
we're all these things,
all of the time and, at least, never, but
everything happens at once.
Born without religion,
birthed by the doorways of battle,
new honey brews its weapons,
is always love-making, and no one asks
if she can keep some hair
for the casket
and let this body grow down
among the weeds of singing children,
anxious to telephone
the world the same, without me here
or with you still in it, awaiting feral.

THE TASTE OF LIGHT & OUR DIGESTIVE TRACTS

I'm portable. My mind travels
the verse and valleys of whole people.
I'm at its heels, the grabbing of long
white trains and veils,
using their hats for sleds.
Africa is one season without snow.
I'm there too, testing the droughts
for true blue under skin cracks
on distant dolphins.
They resemble, in their back fins,
the arc of my casual elbow.
The others I follow also house animals.
The white hair on this front-row man
hides a pink flamingo.
Moustache: a salt & pepper mole rat.
The red-haired woman has antlers
for feeling. So much to throw away
and make space for
the other parts of us: the hole in
my hope,
my tribunal relationships,
the incredible ways we eat baked
goods. It's not possible to enjoy
a bite and set it free before
the swallow. The throat, conditioned,
wants completion.
The stomach demands its vision.
Sweet taste is an evolution,
an attribute.
Go, ask the miracle fruit.
Tell your doctor who pales to kill
my parasites, speak of my inner family.
We have talked on all fours

and succeeded in mastering
the secrets of flexing upright
without destroying
our buried interests. People are friends,
as are all animals. In memory of this,
I bake them into shapes and a spoon-
shaped cake to taste the world with.

MY LOVE ISN'T

Love the way you keep it:
I'm a child when it comes
to sickness,
I've been in diapers
for a year now
wishing for mom's
correction of
the misuse my guts
charge my heart with
racing every time I
turn the corner
to sleep and awaken
half past the past,
broken with ills
that clamor at
needles
knitting out limbs
to stay warm within,
wrap around
a lantern love lit,
torso fire cage
on the water rolling
the ribs' stalling eye
through lips that spell
souls dragging
freshly-hewn people
down parchment streets
in inches
we crawled yesterday's
terrors against,
along a stitched-up horizon
who smiles

back at palms
that speak stigmata
when piercing becomes
us, our very boots
we dance rifts in
until our feeble beats read
names tattooed
on the sleeve's
inner beast: Be &
be not afraid, O kindred.

HYMN FOR THE MISBEGOTTEN

Not heightened, but evaporated,
so goes the chain of my being:
the thinning out of form
puts me in body-time.
I become one more format
for the pleasures of God.
The misamplified edge of God's sin.
Is there such a place as his mistake?
If he made us from dust,
which is his own mildew lifted
where his skirts have passed,
then why not the need for errors
to make things perfect?
I am but one gravity in the jumbled
pull of egrets and sparrows
divining wires for land. Bombs
set us rotating at fast distance, but
the imploding strain
on the elastic waist
of this green planet strips
the universe into pillow books
& incestuous closure again.

Give it some time. Plant a clock.
See if it doesn't find your wallet
between moments. Come together,
unclasp hands, walk apart.
Watch the rain bury its ocean's pockets.
Wear a tulip, pass her seeds
to the field she birthed her lost children in.
She grows there each season,
and after the sod has pulled root up,
the prodigal transplant renews its vows

to wind, who trips along
among the blind, the sighted,
never to speak her true hues aloud.
Eat up to embrace all that we do,
how we pedal and love and put trash
in containers that find
us out in sleep. We engage the zippers
and padlocks sealed to omit
the parts of salvation we think don't need us.

We rise in the bulbs of night
to build our crosses and tie ourselves
to rosaries that balance
out what we think we'll never need:
an eternal bladder of forward motion,
as if the past is swallowed down
in hatch-marked echoes,
gathered to stones
of our walking weight in visions
among his skirts, the blemished rainbows
and tarnished trout that drain
the mouth-torn prayers
of his newborn words,
however absent freewill burns.
We know our purpose as we know
the air trims desire's motion:
the way we leap the tear-soaked armpit
we call God's love & swim into his abandon.

HOW I GOT TO RUSSIA'S KNAPSACK

I bought two yaks
but ate three, whole,
emptied of
my brain is its own head,
unsatiated hyena where
the water futures itself.
How can you rob the lie?
You can, and this is the one
testimony suicides fly to.

We are, so called, rolling
in the snowball wind—
We want sweet song and sighs
(on the hyper side),
a diorama of days
sounding boss out of work,
an underlying worker awake
in the respiratory regions,
slumber beneath sleep
criminals each person
that tells us out,
our fears and their arms,
how we protect
faces not our own
that cameo our dreams'
grey stables, the bucking horses.

What is the smell of vegetables dying?
We ride the balancing vine
as village templates who
seldom murmur our coordinates out,
and I, the familiar weightless

America, am
the laboratories of bodies
whinnying pharmacies,
the dog licking for a piece
of clean flesh:
shall I serve him in a teacup?
The giant holograms of homes
loom in these photos too
even as money's banks slide
wrist-deep into the soup's
porous ground. Duma mir.

WHEN THE BREAD IS IN MY BODY

When the bread is in my body,
I tend to leave you
for the Sioux
in the low lying mother
I grew up on. You're alone
now, a distance from bones
I used to walk upon,
the ones I carry in brown paper
parcels tied with hair from estates,
gone defunct in overgrown
cotton and snakes that would
rattle if their bellies were younger.
My ghost leaning watches
from her rotten woodpile,
sips the head off a beer, &
of course, the dough becomes
another beast I yawn
to let go of. It needs an easy out.
We all do as much
in the process of sheets,
clothes and carpets. We pass extra
history on the way out with
our ducking ways and latchings onto.
We do hook work, portray
a pretty weave, pretend
against the one-eighth rule
of red or black in the seat of skin
who fought the war to keep a status;
I am duty's brick thrown
at the heart of future's pots, sorrow's
kitchen licking yeast from
faces that poke time's back hot.

My eyes are heavy
but my heart is not.
My heart is now.
I take the corners of your mouth,
lead you into pastures
of mules into men in books
you've overlooked on flea market
tables and shelves of families'
homes you've never stepped into.
The dead footsteps pass around
us, crush the beetle meat
of fallen trees and strip the hides
from too-slow rabbits,
those who grew a living field
where wheat still stretches
and bodies buried breathe
into bodies living on
those with bread and flesh enough,
and the talk of time to grow upon.

Act IV

I do not move.
That is what I used to do, weighing everything down.

STATE OF A NATION

The actor is a second life
of people drawn
on the achievable with fiction.
The characters are fleeting
when an actor's flame
blows the shortest immortality.
As a result, great achievements
are limited to audience.
But the audience pants on.
Saliva glows on the mouths'
cornered sounds.
We might live five hundred years
on time's sandbags
that prick with passivity's angels.
They hole our breath and weight us.
The stage baits.
Lungs blow over liver-grey streets.
No one's name survives
some small comfort
though hope will surely be given
ever after. Even after,
we still live in the present.
We live as presidents.
We hold on to the value
of a vote, a soliloquy, a sword,
and the lights after curtain.
Ten thousand years and the barrier
between inner and outer,
grape skin and meat,
sticks marred by grey matter.
That lives will dine at single tables
fermenting veins that push

against wine and palate, seat and vision,
the drive to behave and
the drive to portray knocks our hearts
in order not to die from these truths,
however tailored and ill-fitted.
The only thing to ask?
When I am a million candles,
be my feet.
When I please
with human crisis,
carry me into your finish.
When the tide waxes bold,
grow roots from the specters
beyond me. When I die,
play the boy on the soul
of that death and use
my memory's mud
to make gods of us from the dust.

JUST TO MIND FUCK

People are ample, and they take
so long through the torso
to bleed another mouth,
where you too take
the trombone shot,
probing the day's potentials
paved in rent:
who wears the pants home?
Moisten me down
with nectar from the sheriff,
give me the law of the land,
the Sick Moon Saloon,
pan in and out on
the progress of fire's candy,
breed me like a Scottie
on your favorite rope chain
hoping for a kinder, gentler world
over cabbage soup & clover petals.
With tears of lilac, throats of ash,
I had a dream
that you scared me & the rest of us.
You were lying beside me
on a hotel bed
with strange people
in another room
watching remotely.
You kept massaging
my feet, you threw your legs
over mine and fell
asleep. I am not
so brave, but you're not as slow
as vocabulary goes.

"Hollow is beautiful" would be
my detective too, so
what you say betrays
I'm not in love,
I don't want sex, real
or just to mind fuck—
but to take
care of the furniture, now
while we lie here, infested.

THE PATH TO ASK

No punch in
the gut. No black then
blue. No guessing or
"pro" antlers.
I look sexy in
clothes. Better
with someone who
knows better.
Armed candy and tanks,
this continent bleeding
from the middle
umbilical out.
Is the horse
hooves on camel backs,
is the store water
stuffed fat. Sweetness,
our floor sweats
the rank of rank,
smells of hierarchy.
Not that you're less
than top. The bottom looks
up. Boil the feet, insert
ivory until hard.
Swallow hard.

YOU BELIEVE IN EVERYTHING

I'm doing work, staying
awake,
thinking lateness, overdue.
I'm trying to eat
the esophageal sphincter,
which keeps
shutting down.
The build up is too much
for my tiny
lapdog throat
to bear out.
I squeal
rib sour,
the blockage
takes comeuppance,
an airway narrows.
I am Poseur; can't get
into community, gulp
hors d'oeurves, sip cognac
as elastically as ecstatic.
There. Now you've
subsumed just how much
I love the way you tune.
Allah, creeps, amen.

MY BRAIN IS ITS OWN HEAD

Like a little princess leaves,
we wonder
where the duplicate girl goes
without her Russian doll,
her self replica, the outdoor soul.
So where's my former hat,
my older spouse extracted
before appliances
were written
off the charts, hung apart
from old-timey things. I'd like to
fall for your refreshing
state of mind,
a half-meted snow
or Annie Oakley statuette
borne by a broken neckline.
For the heel of her fingernail
sway, we will eat
dry deer as a holy snack food
& the sun just to hear
my new favorite object
typed apart by sight:
"Will you sing your hyena hymn?"
Okay instead, feel
the edge of an enamel
heart, her creamy hardshell skin
that cinches us in—
She's the one who disappeared
from the earlier mentioned
soon-to-be queen,
foretelling the evils of men:

RADIO SLEEP

Living in the midst
of pupils-up-the-sleeve,
I mean real rabbits, dirtier
than before,
we became our water's
future supply.
We futured the water.
At the onset of correctable
vision, I heard you
flow in a voice decidedly low,
so much so
that they gaze down
the valley and cite
the bull's eye of Sunday,
a victim's warming gallbladder,
open moors of thoroughfares
at the tips of nerves,
the useless eyes.
We were damaged
with disrepair,
the body replacing itself
with paper lanterns
of shadow bones
on a midnight kite
chasing penance and prayer.
I'd given myself sideburns
by then where none
had collected,
rather than listen to an angel's
wings glued loosely
to radio prayers.
Who else will make

the time capsule pass,
quick as skeletons,
small as thunder,
pools where wild horses ride?
We are in the wall
of democracy a balm
to defend the mirror against—
an ostrich never
buries her head or an egg
without fables
to tell the truth against:
When Russians used pencils,
we developed pens
at great cost,
just as a secret portrait
connects every landscape
in us too,
but we hold out
for stapled words
on syntax & grammar
to draw these maps apart.
The prize-giving rowboat
with flailing fingers dips
puddles of vaccinated cheer.
Without the sun's right arm,
I become one less limb
on the face of insight,
melting broken crimson
shards thin enough
to flex the world against.
Soon everyone
will behold themselves
with serrated teeth
that tear us out,
sacred fissures in folds of flesh
meeting skies on sea.

WHEN CATHOLIC GIRLS GO RIDING

My Mexican pony
turned again and found
himself adrift amidst
the Bambis of the Eastern shore.
North Carolina is just
as lovely this time of year,
with soft brown eyes that look
the same as air.
I ride along, forgetting
my comb, so I need
to find a pattern
for an A-line skirt.
Has your dad only
got one eye?
What's he left
to see the rest with?
On the other side
of other words,
you can't tie a person
down with nylon pure.
You can break them out
in corduroy patterns.
You can house them in
with herringbone.
I don't usually take to
women with leisure class
sports jackets.
So if I was overheard
in stating, "I'm going
to buy a massive ring
with conflict diamonds,"
would you admit
our liaisons?

Do you like
my paisley-serged seams
with turquoise ribbon trimmings?
You could truly become
my only glue,
with a touch of open destiny.
Except, I don't
believe in disbelief,
ever the hushed-out cop.
Whatever you do,
don't be yourself instead.
Forego the silence and solitude.
Pull on this chocolate brown
wool appliqué, fully lined.
With each attempt,
she dropped his body
like an acorn's leaf,
a loaf of sugar melted
into hardened human limbs.
Cancer hadn't taught us
anything by then.
Now, the rictus spreads
into my nasal areas.
But I'm wearing this bib
of rib-stitched Gold Lamé
with self yoke and peekaboo
creases that deplete
the injuries my keeper keeps
crossing out.
I'm sure I've worn
my welcome down,
but I kick his sides,
driving across these frictions
on my dearest mule,
sad to leave some beside

the ocean's curbside,
along the road to hell,
one stop after heaven's
gated chartreuse.
God nervously awaits
on the other side
in her mocha acetate
A-line with hand-dyed lace,
and subtle snake bows
tugging at the hemline.

SUCH LIGHT LEADS

The occasional torso
and limb are as occasional
as the common misfit—or
are as common as the occasional?
From whatever end, sleep well,
dear pony who rejoices
to hear that no disaster
has accompanied the first morning
gestures, when flies begin
to stir an essentially tragic ape
who refuses to take
on tragically the merit
of his own rejections
at coffee, juice, meats and cheeses.
Dear anxious brown-
throated cricket, I open
my chest's isolation,
a bare cliché of chirping
kidneys hidden; the ant factories
produced there are aloof too,
imitating most common enemies,
crawling through sleeves
of pilgrims, dilettantes
that whine with friendly wind,
welted mariners too swell
with spring's maroon,
preparing tomorrow
and the remaining mental
cologne you spoke at me
in the brio of grief.
Even then, the empty kidneys
were found
moving freely about the cabin

as in so many procedures
of the patented body: arms & legs,
restless artifacts,
taken on the chin
in fractured fabrics
that sleep in an exchange
of happy cancers
prone to winning.
You imagine the zones
of transubstantiation,
a calico sky in an earlobe's kerchief
that jumps at the window
with a hardened din
of antagonists hidden,
growling the low of low,
souffléd and applied
lengthwise to your see-through
mirror, your spike in appetite
for criminal anima—
You want wolves with beards?
What about little lambs
that live to slaughter?
My right to be lonely?
Or self-arrangement?
Riding an agenda
of static-free confetti,
tell them we spoke "Sayonara"
with our tongues affixed
to the smallest god; there is no zero.
I too will settle
for material-sealed time,
where knitting you was
the most regulatory fun,
after our mutual pony rides, to date.

BLEED ANOTHER MOUTH

Yes, I'm doing this talking
as an arm reaches out
from plastered-on words,
leftover on a plate
of pork fat and greased potatoes
sunk through a sea below
the reaches of ankles,
dull hooks, and coffee punctured
floats into hardened coral,
an ossified limb some jetty
past pig-like remorse
for circumstance culled
in oceanic programming
that misleads
our audience not quite tied
to the running board
of a hazmat jalopy
five thousand knots from being
united with me onto you,
and I'm still degrees
above a distressed canary's
dusty yellow in its agro coal mine,
even more miles over
an iguana who knows no one besides
I told you once, I'll research
a robbery again:
Language is the arm of behavior,
a tongue mustard causing sway,
belly dances,
circumstance of plush-crushed red,
rose-hued tentacles grabbing
the ends of velveteen minutes
that feel like normal in

exchange for us,
the "we" bereft
we come upon
on moldy dark stools
in backroom encounters,
sexless winter now,
summer's backroom of progress,
wine of the bathmat bare
sounding songs
on Halloween vowels,
or starlit Christmas
decorations in utero, such as more
than signatures, we are a species,
a curtain call hurling
voices, thinking you
were among them too,
annexed til delivered.
The next day faded
from brown hairs limbed,
Michelangelo turning crosshairs
to sunshine, people moving on,
and instead of anything,
these soft bodies
make good lovers breaking ground.

EVERYTHING BEGAN WITH AN AXE

Half lit with half light
in twilight tonight,
cutting nicotine twice,
a valiant disguise
that people remark
or rely upon the blackened
bright habits
of their executioners.
Only by a miracle of dying
dinner bells did you
eventually photograph
this sprayed-on dream,
an opinion built
of supply & demand;
but where you go walking,
I write tele-scripts
for tomorrow's play
date-in-progress. We
both grow bowling pin legs
turned toy nightgowns
that spin in Goya paintings
across each other's brow,
nose and lips to hint
at genetic clumsiness.
Even God is dangerously
close in orchestrated larvae
that breathe and teeth
that smoke,
abundant as split potatoes
looking similar
to her swollen version
of your abdomen who turns

outwardly famous
as the people you squirrel
within yourself, famous as
whales beaching
that most basic of elements:
a boiling water
of the second fetal skin.
Now watch me turn
into your intimate book
from whence you will
play the baby bunny back
into swaddling blankets
the color of wheat, a flour
spreading the rest of us
shackled down
in a false-bottom hat,
bubbling with whispered-out
appetites, waiting to be plucked.

Act V

They can because they think they can.

ANARCHY'S TIPTOE

Who's to say what magic
is when we've got vistas
to explore? We'll spend a day
at the Hindu temple,
watch a man who loses everything
still hold his hands
like being married.
A younger man dreams
of lions, a cave, an imminent
slaughter the Lord
intervenes on. His voice took
the sword from my hand,
pardoning ballistics.
I steal ballet from a brandy flask
in the midst of biblical highways.
I had to meet you
crying though, which is often called
"cutting it close".
What has all this to do with us?
Ultimately, a few drops,
regardless of stories told,
get to sparkle
on the cup's quiet rim.
The lying puppet then
bounced into my arms,
and suddenly, I was a mother.
A massage specialist on the next
seat over tapped
her cloven hoof to a single beat
and remembered
Santa Claus out loud.
Long ago

when the world chirped on,
my father and I lived
in an airport. The girl back then
could barely lift her head
to nod at traveling villagers;
she was too small to reach
the ledger to print her name upon.
They called her "Christmas"
in honor of northern stars
falling down around me,
lifting us to a safer place
like an old Parisian house
covered by vines where
twelve more girls lived
in two very straight lines.
My lovelier brothers acquired
the nicknames of Big and Little Dippers.
Divest your interest in
how men are the new women.
Plagued by family
when the house was wild,
a tight corset wouldn't pinch
the waistlines nor squeeze
the chests into pails with shovels.
My grandmother was a gambler
from Holland like Baby Mountain
wandered the banks of the Seine.
Our theaters and music halls drew
passing widows who sang
from these pleated hills.
They housed small Dutch dolls
with black-brown eyes
the color of shiny marmite.
But after twilight, sleep
became an awakening—
our antique shop is very still now.

Usually no one goes
close enough to notice
the noise of biding time,
a vastly off-white habit
from patience.
Enclosed in this forgotten basement,
the galaxy is an awfully big place,
and I am still feeling
the walks between steps,
drowning in part,
footed forever with this forever
project of waking up.

THIS OCEAN

This crutch is smooth corners
and shady leaves of fervent grapes
for the ease of your dialectic.
Scratch that. This worm is not
what it dies from: a note of key
that opens the very rib cage
by which you invite earth's mildew
out. No, again, I admit: this mouth
should be what should be
becomes—what could
have been, had someone admitted
the mysterious "people"
in lines of bees and our shoes
that go one clubbed another
with hurry and fear and thorny
forays into daring dubbed
moments of love, the sentence
that gets you beyond your
head-burnt commercial script,
telling your you-ness just
what a prisoner hopes to implode
with, but despite what I tell
you, that's just it: this anchor isn't.

DRESSING THE WAY

It's easier to wear
what your mother told you
would be the death
of your tiny days
should you not grant her
complete immortality
with your smaller soul power,
barefoot
for what it betrays:
the torso hot with mistaken
escapes. You watched
ants carry her
bloody puddles off,
back to summer cabins and
the queen's hut bound
by a loose dirt hill.
You longed to reduce this world
to the exact moment
fleshy bits became too
large for an ant-size meal.
You are also marrow
coordinates
I hold in a blurring envelope,
every object in purpose
stolen by those
less vested
with the window of plenty,
the permission of superior
phonemes
that crawl
with a mutated ear, not
superior
into the past,
only asking we see
a sideways path
that keeps us safe and criminal.

WHEN THE BRUISE BEGINS TO FLATTER

If the concept of God has any validity or any use, it can only be to make us larger, freer, and more loving. – James Baldwin

I stay here,
a clamorous organ tuning
its lakes into puddles.
My loyalty was one less,
was not a sign of greed
or a caution flag in yellow.
Dear volunteer of salvation,
Is ours negotiation
or are the pamphlets
like weather falling apart:
fat crows, rain heavy
with dead
killing buckshot skies?
You are my sleep
wherever you go,
but will you behave
the oxygen's parenthesis?
When we first began
impersonating antlers,
we were everywhere;
now the forgiveness I read in bed
will finally masquerade
as ghosts at weapons,
the details squirreled by life.
In this country, I thrum between
postures I heal from
and postures you pose in.

THIS WORD WAS NOT IN ANY DICTIONARY

Nothing in the wood
all stacked,
two women spent
in kitchen's yard,
a tractor passing
releases daybreak
with heaving
chests in rest now
press the fishbones
of morning's nest.
Bury this word
silent in us
head-down at
earth's applause—
And work the land,
we sticklers for
the carnivorous lamb,
we tender for
taxes at the door.

THE NATURE OF NATURE

A newspaper dress,
please don't mock
my noise, my rustle,
the scripts of my plot,
these chrysanthemums,
zinnias in flight
attached to a blanket
of humidity's film,
the legs of a beetle
on the sun's full larvae
that say as much
as we fruit that contend
with gravity's puppets,
an apotheosis of gratitude
in the blue stone pot
set to boil
on our borrowed
butterfly stove—
God's straight line
starlit and prone
working the fields,
flickers to see by,
to slow down on,
to pass the nights without.

EDEN

Beneath cabbage wings I lie,
attending midnight.
Your garden breathes.
Such spongy soil bed
enfolds & opens—
earthworms poke my legs,
knee high socks,
a way in.
This delinquent disguise
as you sleep away,
air-conditioned strip
of earth behind
burnt building, Brooklyn
sidewalk and me,
lost weed, skulled
tulip with scalloped eye.
A view to escape within.

FROM THE GIRL BECOMES

The sense that longs
for the sense behind

To believe
a scarecrow's resurrection,

You must, at first, behold the thing
alive.

Follow rusted iron lattice
through a humid English garden—

A dire pond, burgeoning roses,
a hazy woman, my loosened sleeves,
a learning to, how she.

Just as
seashell cried into seashell's ear,

On the greening limbs of
petals' breath, a sleep on tree-ring blanket.

This crawl space narrows
as the child emerges

Ever more fractal,
ever more motion.

WE ARE GREAT SONGS

A child touched the sweet faint
bulb of a pale green tongue.
Aqua blew out
the eyes of impossibility.
She shocked herself into scene,
tasting chalk blown sky of rabbit tails,
tall firs with opal ocean swaying
the horizon's waistline.

That the essence of the famous
phrase, "I'll never finish taking off
all of these masks" attempts to apply
the history of madness
to the craft of enlightenment,
we each, in death, now chase
a perfect example of violence
into gusts of dust kicked
beforehand: borrowed tales.

We are great imitators. We walk
with a child's hand held,
even if only as our own imprint,
looking for the lightest patch
of vanity's peach and the darkest
reptile head beneath
a swollen sea log
to peer out at us.
We are innocent in the depths
of our guilt. Such sin is
an anchor that misreads success.

Honey also has no natural

divisions and is instantly
in place, is always
the marriage of sap into shape.
The young tongue laps
what's molten, immodest.
Enter the decipherer. Play opens
up to what we want
to be doing. Liquor unlocks
adult substitutes. We keep on
living in the shambles
of America, cowless people
loving the feel of machines
and how we bathe nudely.

Like people, I'm a stranger
here now, squarely out
of pivot—but if I stand still
enough, motionless, I begin
to belong. As much as anyone,
Brooklyn remains busy in
its torments, its gashes, its faint array
of willing and rebellious tenants.
The shock of every foot
and leash and child passing
ripples through atoms we think
we own. With or without the calm
of knowing. I sip my neighbor,
her homegrown coffees.

The body's prospects turn proteins
into peptides and bacterium
to carbon. We cleanse the other like
the moon is replete
in her remembrance pool:
our memoirs in broken lines
of the people she is

and the people she sweetens. She thinks,
First I will cut the heads
with artificial fire, study
the Igbo tribe's inflections
to learn what it means to be
elsewhere, while history stands
a volcano in Pompeii,
burying village mores,
stone-gripped and frosted glass.

That's what she thought once.
In echo, I opened the gullet
of my brain to ask,
Is it real that I am
the palpitations that come
at intermittent pace now,
because I know the woman
beside me is not my Michele,
my French star to the stars,
a minoring pageant?
In fact, no one is lying
down and my guts' snakes plunge
into plodding gulps,
upset and heart threatening.

The bed stays indented and warm,
the prior person rattles glass
milk bottle in our moonglow
kitchen. I see her down the hall
with orbing halo
around her cotton white gown.
I am taken, beaten out.
She, or I, could be anyone
in this studio Provence.
Earlier that morning, seated
at the village café, we watched heat
rise from cobblestones.

This could be New York or ringside.
I said to myself, like saying to her,
Sing for the love you bring.

She stole her mouth then,
turned hummingbird,
shot electric, which doesn't
linger but is the dry
vinegar of each being's fluid.
I've managed to hurt my hands
since then in a number of ways
through this process of venture,
held them out for the count
at the passing years.

So down a swift hill
as the insects hide
in the still before sky.
With the rain came song.
This hill is not metaphor,
the imprint of hill
holds a papyrus-cinched slope,
the paper scene of ink release
is actual, a literal exchange
we reach across
a coconut void,
drops between lightning,
to a face on the placard,
looking down
the hill that tilts
by the pen's own angle,
prodigious, same degree,
same lilt as the green
pearl in silt,
telling your tongue
that licks my scent dry.

We have come fully
round to the child again,
her hands, our love, this art,
the gaze that watches
us leave things out, a story
untold, partial life implied,
just as a crime
is not about the final goods
or sentence stricken,
but turns out to be
the cost of plunging
every ounce of gold
that drove you
to the brink of security,
to toe beneath logs, speak
leviathan orbits, hold
out for missing persons,
sketching lines
that reckon the dead,
untying wrists
you know aren't yours,
not in name or by word
but by the jugular
of an etched-over dream that
you bare them with,
Goliath inspired
by gibbous oceans &
opal tree lines, happy, in fact.

NOTES

Act I – "The soul that suffered from being its body" – poem title from <u>Cesar Vallejo / The Complete Posthumous Poetry</u> translated by Clayton Eshleman and Jose Rubia Barcia.

Act II – "Growing up spoiled a lot of things." -- Betty Smith, <u>A Tree Grows in Brooklyn</u>.

Act III – "Selling one's soul to God: is to betray the Other." --Claude Cahun, <u>Disavowels</u>.

Act IV – "I do not move. / That is what I used to do, weighing everything down." – from "These Tall Constructions" by Dora Maar (translated by Mary Ann Caws).

Act V – "They can because they think they can." Virgil, <u>The Aeneid</u>.

From "We Are Great Imitators" – "I'll never finish taking off all of these masks." Claude Cahun, <u>Disavowels</u>.

From "From the Girl Becomes" – "*seashell cried into seashell's ear.*" "No Dove" by Günter Grass.

Amy King is the author of **I'm the Man Who Loves You** and **Antidotes for an Alibi**, both from Blazevox Books, **The People Instruments** (Pavement Saw Press Chapbook Award), and forthcoming, **I Want to Make You Safe** (Litmus Press). She teaches English and Creative Writing at SUNY Nassau Community College and, with Ana Bozicevic, curates the Brooklyn-based reading series, The Stain of Poetry. For more information, please visit <u>amyking.org</u>.

Made in the USA
Charleston, SC
15 March 2010